Arctic Ocean

Alaska

WITHDRAWN

Canada

Atlantic Ocean

United States

Pacific Ocean

Mexico

Ian McAllister and Alex Van Tol

Great Bear Rainforest

A Giant-Screen Adventure in the Land of the Spirit Bear

ORCA BOOK PUBLISHERS

Cataloguing in Publication information available from Library and Archives Canada

Issued in print and electronic formats.

ISBN 978-1-4598-2279-5 (hardcover).—ISBN 978-1-4598-2280-1 (pdf).—ISBN 978-1-4598-2281-8 (epub)

Summary: A companion to Ian McAllister's film for IMAX® and giant-screen theaters, *Great Bear Rainforest*.

IMAX® is a registered trademark of IMAX Corporation.

Simultaneously published in Canada and the United States in 2019
Library of Congress Control Number: 2018962236

MIX
Paper from
responsible sources
FSC® C016245
www.fsc.org

Orca Book Publishers is dedicated to preserving the environment and has printed this book on Forest Stewardship Council® certified paper.

Orca Book Publishers gratefully acknowledges the support for its publishing programs provided by the following agencies: the Government of Canada, the Canada Council for the Arts and the Province of British Columbia through the BC Arts Council and the Book Publishing Tax Credit.

Design by Rachel Page
Image management by Deirdre Leowinata
Front cover photos: Deirdre Leowinata (top), Ian McAllister
Back cover and flap photos: Ian McAllister
Interior photos:
Stills from the film: 1, 2-3, 4-5, 8, 12-13, 20, 22-23, 35, 39, 40-41, 52-55, 59, 62-65
Ian McAllister: 6-7, 10-11, 14-16, 19, 21, 25, 28, 30-34, 36-38, 42-45, 47, 56-58, 60, 70, 73, 75, 85-88
Deirdre Leowinata: 9, 17, 26-27, 29, 46, 48-49, 50-51, 61, 66-67, 71-72, 76-83
Andy Maser: 18
Devin Card: 68-69, 74 (TOP)
Brian Dalrymple: 75, 84
Adrian Samarra: 91
Haley Crozier: 74 (RIGHT)

About the photographs:
All of the images in this book are of wild animals in wild circumstances.

ORCA BOOK PUBLISHERS
orcabook.com

Printed and bound in Canada.

22 21 20 19 • 4 3 2 1

We have a belief, in all of our work, that what we have
here is not ours. It belongs to future generations.
And my Elders have always stated that if you take
care of the land, the land will take care of you.

—Douglas Neasloss, Chief Councillor,
Kitasoo/Xai'Xais Nation

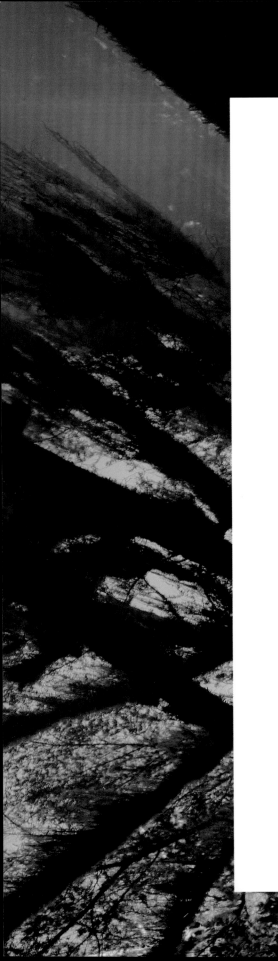

CONTENTS

Heiltsuk First Nation territory.

Introduction

IN THE NORTHWEST CORNER of British Columbia, between Alaska and the northern tip of Vancouver Island, lies a land of forest green and sparkling blue. From the vast schools of silver herring to the massive grizzly bears, this place is home to an immense array of wildlife.

This is the Great Bear Rainforest: misty, lush, wild, abundant. It rains most of the time in this coastal paradise; the falling water washes clean the trees and plants and mosses, soaks the roots deep in the dark soil and makes the forest fresh for each new day.

Life abounds here.

Measuring 6.4 million hectares—about the size of Ireland or Nova Scotia—the Great Bear Rainforest is one of the wildest places on Earth. It supports the largest tract of intact temperate rainforest left on the planet. Only about 18,000 people live in the Great Bear today. Some twenty-six First Nations have called this coast home for well over 10,000 years. The forest's human residents live in small towns like Bella Bella, Kitimat, Klemtu and Hartley Bay.

Getting from one place to another in the Great Bear Rainforest isn't as easy as hopping in a car. In fact, most of the towns and villages are accessible only by boat or float plane. This makes it a difficult place for people

Estuaries provide critical food for coastal grizzly bears.

Temperate rainforests are one of the rarest forest types in the world.

to visit. It's also one of the main reasons why it's so wild. But even remote places like the Great Bear Rainforest face an uncertain future as more and more of the world's natural resources are harvested.

While some adventurous travelers have visited this rainforest to see the rare white spirit bear—and others to hunt its black and grizzly cousins—it has been challenging to share this place of beauty and bounty with the outside world.

With this in mind, in 2016, work began on the filming of *Great Bear Rainforest.* A longtime passion project of photographer and conservation leader Ian McAllister, the film took almost twenty years to complete, from shaping the initial idea to shooting the last IMAX® reel.

"We are a visual species," says Ian, "and as a conservationist I have always believed that visual storytelling is one of the best ways to inspire people to protect a place."

Working with a skilled team of filmmakers, producers, audio and video experts, First Nations, helicopter and drone pilots, deckhands and crew members, Ian has made his dream of sharing this exquisite place with the world come true. "The challenge of making a film for the massive IMAX screen is considerable in the most predictable and staged situations," Ian says. "But attempting one in such a remote landscape with some of the most elusive wildlife on the planet elevates it to a whole new level."

Now the Great Bear Rainforest is accessible to everyone, in exceptional, immersive quality on the giant screen.

Come. Enter. Enjoy. Learn and delight. Be awed, and see for yourself why this untamed outpost—fragile, wild, unbroken—is worth preserving.

BRINGING THE GREAT BEAR TO THE GIANT SCREEN

Ian carried the idea of the *Great Bear Rainforest* film around for nearly twenty years, pitching it to whoever would listen. He knew that the best way to improve conservation in the rainforest would be to put the story right in front of people's eyes. "There is no other format that could do justice to a place like the Great Bear Rainforest," he says, "other than on a giant screen with twelve-channel sound that really showcased its grandeur and scale."

Chest waders (big waterproof overalls) are an essential equipment item for director Ian McAllister and his crew.

SNAPSHOT: IAN MCALLISTER

Born and raised: Victoria, BC

Home base: Most often on his boat, *Habitat.* When he's not on the boat, Ian migrates between an island in the Great Bear Rainforest and the Cowichan Valley on Vancouver Island.

Professional handle: Photographer; filmmaker; executive director of Pacific Wild, a wildlife conservation organization operating in the Great Bear Rainforest

Work history: Standing up for BC's unprotected places; co-founder of Pacific Wild; photographing and filming the wildlife of the Great Bear Rainforest so that others can see and understand the importance of preserving this pristine wild area

When the bug bit: In his teens, when his dad, Peter, became interested in conservation. Ian first joined his father in 1988 at a logging blockade in Clayoquot Sound, BC, spending his first night as a protester hoisted high in a basket over a logging road.

Role in making the film: Director, filmmaker, diver, climber, captain, coffee drinker

Soft spot: Coastal wolf packs—and his own pack made up of his wife, Karen, and their children, Callum and Lucy

Approximate number of shots muffed during filming: "Millions"

Most recent victory: Capturing footage of surf scoters (seabirds) feeding on herring eggs underwater after three years of trying

Pet peeves: Leaky dry suits and dead batteries

Claims to fame: 11 books; helping to end the grizzly bear trophy hunt in BC; turning the world's attention to the Great Bear Rainforest

A black bear with a successful catch of a coho salmon.

But even if he had been successful in securing support for the movie back in the early 2000s, the film equipment then was huge and awkward—even more so than it is today. (IMAX film magazines are the largest in the world, because the film is twice the size of traditional movie film—70 millimeters instead of 35 millimeters—to capture the quality needed for the IMAX screen.) "The cameras were very big, heavy and loud," Ian says, referring to the equipment available twenty years ago. "I just couldn't see how we could possibly film wildlife in a non-invasive manner—the bears would run for the hills once those big old cameras started up."

Fast forward to 2014, when the Great Bear Rainforest was slowly becoming recognized as one of the planet's natural wonders. One afternoon, Ian met with Kyle Washington, who was interested in learning more about Pacific Wild's work. Over lunch, Kyle told Ian how excited his children had been after seeing an IMAX film. The conversation soon turned to the opportunity to make an IMAX film of the Great Bear Rainforest as a way to raise awareness of this important piece of the world—and Kyle agreed.

By the time Kyle and his family came on board, smaller and quieter digital cameras that could deliver IMAX-quality images were becoming available. Ian and his crew were able to field-test some brand-new digital technology in making the movie. "In order to capture elusive, rarely documented wildlife behavior, it meant being quiet and somewhat mobile in the field," Ian says. "It was super exciting that the technology had finally caught up."

A mother grizzly and her yearling cub.

DID YOU KNOW?

Putting the *Great Bear Rainforest* IMAX together was a huge job, not just on the ground but also in the editing room. Think about it: three years of filming and recording the awe-inspiring wildlife and landscapes of this coast, from the underwater world and across the vast rainforest archipelago to the very tops of the Coast Mountain range. Add to that the deep human history in this part of the world...and it all had to be jammed into forty-one minutes—the standard length of an IMAX film.

Harbor seal glides through a forest of kelp.

In the Water

Pink salmon waiting for the rains so they can migrate upriver.

At maturity salmon return to the stream where they were born. They migrate upstream together in an impressive event called a salmon run. After they spawn, laying and fertilizing eggs, they die.

WHEN YOU FIRST LEARN ABOUT the Great Bear Rainforest, you'll likely hear about the salmon. All five Pacific species—chum, coho, sockeye, pink and chinook—call the Great Bear home. They hatch in the shallow waters of the Great Bear's riverbeds and then head for the ocean, where they spend between two and seven years growing up. Well, except sockeye: these fish spend a year or so in a freshwater lake before they make the trek to the open ocean.

At maturity, the salmon return to the same stream where they were born. They migrate upstream together in an impressive event called a salmon run where the spawn by laying and fertilizing eggs. Then they die.

More than 2,500 salmon runs take place in the Great Bear Rainforest each year, in the hundreds of river valleys that slice through the coastline. Depending on the species, the salmon runs usually begin sometime in August and can end as late as November. Each run lasts about forty days. No matter how big and strong the fish may be when they start their journey homeward, the run is exhausting. The salmon have to swim

SCIENCE BYTE:
Salmon Navigation

Salmon don't use Google Maps, yet rarely do they get their directions wrong and enter a different stream than the one they were born in. Scientists aren't sure how salmon are able to navigate back to the same spawning ground in which they hatched. Maybe it's chemical cues. After all, fish have been shown to have an excellent sense of smell, and each river valley has its own distinctive aroma. Alternatively, the salmon's homing mechanism might have something to do with Earth's magnetic field. Sockeye salmon have a small amount of iron in their skulls, which might play a role in helping them use Earth's magnetism to navigate home.

Spirit bear—one of the rarest bears in the world—fishing for salmon.

DID YOU KNOW?

A keystone species gets its name from the center stone at the top of an archway. A keystone locks all the other stones in place—an arch cannot be self-supporting until the keystone is placed. Herring may be considered a keystone species because they feed almost everything else in the Great Bear Rainforest, including salmon. Salmon too can be considered a keystone because along with feeding bears and wolves and whales, their decaying carcasses post-spawn serve to fertilize the trees and the estuaries. Both salmon and herring can be considered not only keystone, but also critical to the health of this ecosystem.

thousands of miles through the ocean and then battle their way upstream against a stiff current to spawn. Sometimes they have to leap through churning waterfalls, up and up and up as they make their way up the streambed.

After having avoided whales, seals and fishing nets in the ocean, now they have to contend with hungry grizzly and black bears lining the riverbanks. Bears of the rainforest eagerly await the salmon's return each autumn. The fish offer so much: protein to build muscle, fat to get them through hibernation and a delicious change from their largely vegetarian diet.

When the fishing's good, the bears can afford to be picky eaters. Typically they eat the fatty parts of salmon, like the skin and eggs. For anything that's left over, there is always a long lineup of animals waiting! When the salmon run nears its end, the bears get less picky and will eat almost every part of the silvery swimmers (except the testes—apparently they're not very appealing to a bear's palate).

The fish also provide essential nutrients to the forest itself. Bears and wolves drag the salmon carcasses into the trees, where they can enjoy their meals without being disturbed. Here, the uneaten parts of the fish—whatever isn't gobbled down by the bears themselves or by scavengers like ravens, gulls and martens—are left on the forest floor to decompose. Carrion flies lay their eggs in the carcasses; thousands of maggots quickly hatch and consume the salmon in only a matter of days. Eventually the maggots pupate into adult flies, providing food for birds and other insects. Sometimes they even end up in the stream, where they become food for fish!

Over time, bacteria and fungi break down the remaining soft tissues of the fish, returning rich nutrients to the soil. The plants and trees can then use those nutrients in microscopic form. Their root systems soak up important elements like nitrogen, which is necessary for photosynthesis.

Because of the salmon's importance to the ecology of the entire Great Bear Rainforest, scientists call it a keystone species. Most organisms living there rely in one way or another on the salmon's presence.

Chum and pink salmon migrate into their natal rivers to spawn.

DID YOU KNOW?

A foundation species supports many other species in an ecosystem—just like the foundation of an apartment building supports the homes inside. In the Great Bear Rainforest, kelp forests are seen as a foundation species, supporting herring and sea otters and young salmon, which in turn support many other creatures.

So you see, salmon are an important part of the Great Bear Rainforest ecology. But there's another, unsung, hero in this coastal story—one that doesn't get the same amount of attention as bigger species like bears, wolves and salmon.

We're talking about the herring. These little fish travel in schools weighing tens of thousands of tons. The herring's springtime return to the Great Bear Rainforest heralds the end of hunger after the long winter season and brings hope for a bountiful and productive year on the coast. Unlike salmon, herring don't die after they spawn; they can spawn six or more times before they reach the end of their lifespan. If conditions are right, each female can lay around 20,000 eggs during the spawning season. They lay the sticky eggs on kelp, sea grass or rocks.

As one of the Great Bear's foundation species, the herring is important to the Heiltsuk First Nation's culture. Not only does the herring spawn mark the beginning of their new year, signaling the end of a long winter, but the eggs (roe) themselves provide a rich source of food. "When the herring come, everything else comes alive," says Saul Brown (Háziłba, pronounced Ach'ebuh), who took part in the filming. "The whales come to feed on them, the wolves, the marine and terrestrial animals come to feed on them...everything comes alive."

Using an underwater scooter, Ian is able to travel quickly and quietly through the Great Bear Sea, filming as he goes.

Pacific herring, the foundation of the coast, migrate inshore before their great spawn.

HEILTSUK ACCEPT THE RESPONSIBILITY OF PROPER STEWARDSHIP.

Heiltsuk First Nation fishers follow the ancient tradition of harvesting herring eggs on hemlock boughs.

The Heiltsuk are careful about how they harvest the herring roe, though. They don't follow industrial commercial fishing practices that kill the adults to extract the roe. They're sensitive to maintaining the balance of the entire ecosystem, and they understand that overfishing one species means causing a disastrous ripple of impacts throughout the whole rainforest. In recognizing that the herring are a gift from the creator, the Heiltsuk accept the responsibility of proper stewardship.

The Heiltsuk have an ancient relationship with herring, and the way they fish for them today is not that different from how their ancestors fished thousands of years ago. For generations, Heiltsuk fishers like Saul have collected roe from lines of kelp or, as you see in the film, hemlock branches placed in sheltered areas along the coast. This allows the people of the rainforest to benefit from the nutritious herring eggs without destroying the whole animal. It's a message they're trying to share with the wider world: creating a more sustainable fishery will benefit both humans and fish alike, and it will also help to rebuild the herring population after decades of destructive commercial fishing.

In the Great Bear, the herring are important to more than just the Heiltsuk people. These sleek silver fish provide a nutrient-dense food source for seabirds, wolves, mink, eagles and black bears, as well as for marine mammals like sea lions, dolphins and humpback whales. A herring school can reach up to several miles in length, so when a bunch of them swim by, it's like a dinner bell for everyone in the water.

CREW QUIP:
It's been scientifically proven that we've occupied this territory for over 14,000 years. That's three times as old as the Pyramids of Giza. That's approximately 700 generations worth of Heiltsuk people living here. We want to ensure that there can be another 14,000 years and another 700 generations' with Heiltsuk occupying these lands and these waters.

—Jordan Wilson

DID YOU KNOW?
Herring are an important food fish for salmon, making up more than half their diet.

Each spring countless species rely on the return of herring—the foundation species of the coast—to the Great Bear Rainforest.

Frank (left) and Saul Brown travel to the herring spawning grounds.

Heiltsuk law essentially instructs its people to speak and act correctly; it's a very different approach than European law, which tells people what they can't and shouldn't do. We try to live in an honorable way, and in a way that is conducive to abundance and sustainability in our territory.
—Saul Brown, Heiltsuk First Nation

Humpback whales will work together to round up huge numbers of herring by swimming in circles below a school and blowing bubbles. The bubbles act like a net (which is why it's called bubble-net feeding). The bubbles spook the fish into staying in the center of the ring of rising bubbles. Once the fish are nicely corralled, the humpbacks lunge toward the center of the herring ball, mouths open to capture as many of the tasty morsels as possible. Sea lions also swim around in the fray, grabbing up mouthfuls of the fish and creating a cacophony of splashing.

GOTTA GET THE SHOT

It was a lot of work for Ian to get a shot of sea lions hunting the herring. First of all, the visibility had to be good. Then of course there had to be herring and sea lions—and it had to happen during daylight hours, because artificial lights would scare the sea lions. So it meant being in the right place at the right time.

Ian and the crew didn't get the perfect shot until the third season of filming, after hundreds of dives. One reason is that during the herring spawn, the water gets churned up pretty quickly with sea lions, birds and whales all jockeying for the best fishing spots, making it difficult to film. Another reason? The poop from thousands of tons of herring can make the water awfully messy!

HAMMERED BY HERRING

You would think that a bunch of little fish wouldn't create more than a ripple. But you'd be wrong. Herring travel in schools that weigh thousands of tons. Such a large traveling band packs an incredible amount of force and power. More than once, Ian was pinned to the bottom of the ocean as a school of herring executed a quick turn nearby. "If they come from behind, you don't know what's happening," Ian says. "It's deathly quiet underneath, and then suddenly it turns dark and it's like being hit by a storm." There have even been documented cases of herring schools tipping over full-sized fishing boats!

CREW QUIP:

Imagine trying to swim through a kelp forest and you've got a 12-foot (3.6-meter) slider with these big long legs on it. Plus this great big camera and a scooter, and you're trying to carry all this stuff through the kelp forest. It's like trying to get through a spiderweb. It gets caught up on everything. Sometimes you just get so tangled and you're like, *What am I doing?*

—Ian McAllister

Ever gregarious Steller sea lions.

Director Ian McAllister films the salmon run.

CATCH ME IF YOU CAN!

Filming salmon in a river is a tricky job. The job gets even trickier when you're trying to capture the perfect shot of a salmon jumping into a bear's jaws...right in the middle of a waterfall!

In the *Great Bear Rainforest* film, the crew used a specialized high-speed camera to capture footage of salmon as they leaped their way over a churning waterfall. This camera technology allows every drop of water to be visible on the giant screen as it bounces off the leaping salmon.

It was a tough location for filming: the rocks were slippery, the river's current was fast, and an underwater vortex at the base of the falls awaited anyone who slipped. On one memorable occasion, Ian was sucked right down into the vortex, camera and all! (Fortunately the crew were able to pull him back up with his safety line.) It took a bit of scrambling—but eventually the team got the shot they were trying for.

THE DELIGHT AND DRUDGERY OF DIVE-TENDING

Much of the underwater filming for *Great Bear Rainforest* took place in winter, when the water was clear. While it's cold for the diver, it's even colder on the surface for the dive-tender. That's the person who goes on the Zodiac with the diver, helps with their gear, follows the diver's bubbles while they're underwater filming and is on hand to help again when the diver surfaces. "In winter, everything gets wet," says Deirdre Leowinata, who was the main field technician and a frequent dive-tender for the *Great Bear Rainforest* filming. "Your hands are soaked. It's the coldest thing ever. As a dive-tender you just sit there in a small boat watching bubbles surface on the top of the water for hours while the divers are in the water. It's not the most glorious job on a film, but it's a critical one."

The crew on *Habitat* traveled more than 7,000 nautical miles over the three-year shoot—or 13,000 kilometers. Deckhand Nicola Shipman held the record for longest day in the wheelhouse (16 hours!).

SAUL BROWN AND HIS FATHER, Frank Brown, are Heiltsuk people living in the Great Bear Rainforest. Descended from a long line of hereditary chiefs, Saul works as a negotiator for the reconciliation process between the Government of Canada and Indigenous people. He's also a herring fisherman, collecting roe from kelp. Much of what Saul knows he learned from his father, and from his grandfather before him, and so on, throughout his family's long history in this region.

The Heiltsuk have lived in these territories for at least 14,000 years—long before European settlers arrived. For centuries they governed themselves and the land they shared with other creatures, keeping a careful balance between what they took and what they gave back. Heiltsuk law essentially instructs its people to "speak and act correctly," says Saul, noting that it's a very different approach from European law, which tells people what they can't and shouldn't do. "We try to live in an honorable way," he says, "and in a way that is conducive to abundance and sustainability in our territory."

Setting up rigs for filming on the water while keeping camera equipment dry was a never-ending task.

From the deck of *Habitat*, Tim Archer (left) and Brian Dalrymple aim their equipment at the Heiltsuk fishers' herring-roe-on-hemlock harvest.

The herring have always been important to the Heiltsuk people, forming a cultural and economic foundation for this rainforest-based community. But that all changed when privately owned companies began logging and fishing in the Heiltsuk's traditional territories, beginning in the mid-1800s. Rivers became filled with silty runoff, and fish spawning beds were destroyed. Too much unsustainable commercial fishing depleted herring and salmon stocks. The Heiltsuk were frustrated and angry, because their land and ways were being destroyed. But their law was not recognized as being as important as Canada's federal and provincial laws—and so their voice was drowned out. They were even forbidden to harvest and hunt with the ecologically sensible methods they had used for thousands of years.

All the First Nations people in the Great Bear Rainforest were badly affected by the arrival of settler society. European colonization changed their lives over the course of a century and a half—and recovering from those changes is proving to be difficult. Coastal First Nations were forced to burn their totem poles and other cultural materials. Tens of thousands died of smallpox, a virus brought by the settlers. They were forced off their traditional territories onto smaller land preserves. Their hunting and

CREW QUIP:

Bubbles are a huge challenge in the underwater world. You expel bubbles and herring just...they're gone, because sea lions expel bubbles. It's kind of a form of aggression, or anxiety at least. So I've learned to go down to the bottom, get stationed and hold my breath. I'll be sitting there and suddenly things start to show up and then the fish are swimming and everyone's happy, but then all of a sudden I blow bubbles...and everything disappears. I hold my breath a lot.

—Ian McAllister

fishing rights were restricted. They were forbidden to conduct Potlatch, a system of feasts and gift-giving that shaped economic and social structures within and between nations. And generations of First Nations children were sent away to Christian residential schools whose job it was to "kill the Indian in the child."

Like many nations, the Heiltsuk never gave up trying to be heard. They pointed out how logging was damaging their territory. They showed how their own ways of harvesting herring were much more sustainable than commercial fishing practices. They continue to fight for their environment and their rights and title.

Now, after so many years, reconciliation is finally on the Canadian government's agenda. The First Nations people are at last being heard.

But there is still much to be done.

YOU NEVER KNOW WHAT'S COMING

Interacting with dozens of large carnivores underwater is all in a day's work for Ian. On more than one occasion a curious sea lion has investigated him very thoroughly, usually by coming up behind him and putting its open jaws over his head. That might sound startling—and it was for Ian the first couple of times it happened. But after years of living in the

Steller sea lions are known to eat more than 50 species of prey, but these large pinnipeds mostly prefer small schooling fish like herring.

Steller sea lions are making a remarkable return to the Great Bear Rainforest after decades of government-sponsored kill programs.

rainforest and learning about their behavior, Ian understands that sea lions often explore their environment with their mouths. "You have this thousand-pound animal putting its jaws over your head and giving a little squeeze, but they're really just trying to feel what it is," Ian says. "You can imagine if they wanted to treat your head like a grape they could, but they don't. They're just curious. You kind of have to just have faith that they're not going to keep pressing."

Ian indeed has that faith, because he realizes two things: First, sea lions are highly intelligent creatures with established natural cycles that don't include humans as a cause of great concern. Second, following on from the first, humans aren't part of their menu. They much prefer fish!

Being able to observe and learn from the sea lions is a rush for Ian. "In the underwater world where we're so clumsy and awkward and vulnerable, it's amazing to have these sea lions, especially the big bull sea lions, moving around like mermaids. Sometimes you can be surrounded by thirty, forty, fifty of them, and they're all trying to feel you with their jaws," he laughs. "I think the closest I've ever been to drowning was just laughing so hard underwater having this happen to me."

The recovery of sea otters is helping to bring back kelp forests and other critical habitat.

EVEN THOUGH THE HERRING FEED many rainforest animals, sea otters have other preferences. These fluffy marine mammals stick closer to shore, where they can hunt and raise their babies in the abundant kelp beds that line the central coast. Most of the time they rest on their backs in "rafts," hanging out with other sea otters. Sea otters will do almost anything on their backs, including sleeping, grooming and eating, using their stomachs as a dining table!

The sea otters you see in the film reflect a coastal success story: hunted to extinction in British Columbia by the early 1900s, they've been able to stage a remarkable comeback after eighty-nine Alaskan sea otters were relocated to the west coast of Vancouver Island between 1969 and 1972.

Now numbering 6,000 individuals in BC waters, the sea otter population has grown more slowly in recent years, as it gets closer to being in balance with the ecosystem (equilibrium). Sea otters are still considered a threatened species and are now protected from hunting in British Columbia.

SCIENCE BYTE:
Neighbors Helping Neighbors

Considered a keystone species, sea otters help keep Pacific kelp forests healthy. These huge forests of bull kelp—a brown algae that anchors to the seafloor and grows up to two feet a day—offer habitat for a diversity of wildlife, including crabs, perch, rockfish and otters. Like other forests, kelp beds capture carbon dioxide from the atmosphere — important ecological work. Sea otters help the kelp do its job by eating sea urchins, one of kelp's key predators.

British Columbia's kelp forests are in good shape, but many other kelp forests around the world have died off due to warming waters.

Sea otter mothers are one of the most dedicated in the animal kingdom.

HOW DO YOU CATCH A HUMPBACK WHALE?

If you've ever gone whale watching, you'll know that finding whales is a difficult task. The ocean is huge—and whales are hidden under the surface!

It was just as difficult for the film crew to anticipate where the whales might appear while feeding on herring. Fairly quickly, though, sound designer Tim Archer figured out a way to alert the team that a group of whales was about to surface. "I had bought a hydrophone for the project," he says. "I'd drop it into the water, probably forty feet (twelve meters) down, and I'd put my headphones on." After some careful listening, Tim picked up on a pattern among the whales' vocalizations that gave clues as to when they might breach. "You hear one, then a second one comes in, and then you hear what I call a bark," he explains. "Then you hear the trumpet. And then...you see them!"

Sure enough, just after they made the trumpeting noise, the whales would crash through the surface of the water, mouths open to swallow as much herring as possible. "And it happened every time exactly the same way," Tim says. "So I was able to say, *OK, guys, I hear one, get the cameras ready...all right...there's the bark...wait for the trumpet. OK, there's the trumpet. Start rolling.*"

Tim was able to tell the crew when to start shooting. What he couldn't tell them was *where*. "So what they would do is they would look and find where the seagulls were going, because the fish were starting to jump," Tim says. "And as soon as they saw the seagulls, all cameras went there. And we nailed it almost every time."

SNAPSHOT: TIM ARCHER

Professional handle: Sound designer

Education: Southern Alberta Institute of Technology in the multimedia film, television and radio program. Originally he thought he'd do music production since he loves music so much, but he switched streams after enrolling. "Picture just hit me over the head when I got into film school," he says. "It was like, *This is what I want to do.*"

Years in the audio business: Thirty-three, both as a studio owner and as a freelance sound designer

Role in making the film: Wandering the forest with his assortment of microphones to capture the sounds (and the snores, screeches and howls) of the Great Bear Rainforest

Happiest times: When he's mixing sound sitting right in the middle of the IMAX theater, in the final stages of production

Secret weapon: Little digital recorders that do as good a job as the bigger, fancier, costlier ones

What keeps him up at night: The high percentage of youth who permanently damage their hearing by listening to loud music using earbuds

Secret identity: Inventor

Humpback whales work together to round up herring in a method called bubble-net feeding.

SCIENCE BYTE:
Humpback Habits

Hunted almost to extinction in the early 1900s, humpback whales are rebuilding their population in the North Pacific. From a low of between 1,400 and 6,000 individuals (estimates vary), these giant mammals now number over 20,000. Nobody is certain why the whales have returned—possibly because these are some of the last quiet waters that provide abundant food.

Humpbacks eat small schooling fishes like herring and krill (a small, shrimp-like crustacean). Instead of chewing with teeth, these giants gulp big mouthfuls of prey and then force the extra water out of their mouth. Special baleen plates in their jaw have hairs that trap small prey items, leaving supper behind.

Humpbacks got their name because of how they dive. When breaching, these gentle giants throw two-thirds of their body out of the water before slapping back down with a mighty splash. Their blow can reach up to ten feet (three meters) in the air!

SEA OTTERS, SEA LIONS, humpback whales, salmon and herring—these are just a handful of species that make up the complex and important web of life in the North Pacific Ocean. It's important for humans to recognize and honor that web by learning more about it and by taking steps to protect it so the Great Bear ecosystem can stay strong and healthy for the future.

So far, only about 5 percent of British Columbia's marine environment is protected by law. "To me this is one of the most beautiful places in Canada," says Douglas Neasloss, who is elected Chief Councillor and resource stewardship director of the Kitasoo/Xai'xais First Nation in the small coastal community of Klemtu. (In the film Douglas works with Mercedes Robinson-Neasloss, a young researcher, to collect and interpret grizzly bear hair.) "Hopefully this film will be able to show that everything from marine life to the land use, everything is connected," Douglas says. "You mess with one, it'll alter everything else."

Graceful and acrobatic, Steller sea lions play in the cold waters of the Pacific.

Western red cedar and hemlock trees are common species of the coastal temperate rainforest.

On the Land

Sibling coastal wolves meet up after a night's hunt.

Coastal wolves swim from island to island in search of prey.

THE GREAT BEAR RAINFOREST enjoys a rich underwater ecology, but what happens on the land is as important as what's going on in the ocean. In this web-of-life relationship, the health of one connects directly to the well-being of the other.

Let's explore that relationship a little. We'll start by looking at the coastal wolves, a species that's genetically different from any other wolves on the planet. Coastal wolves—or sea wolves, as they're often called—are smaller than the wolves on the other side of the Coast Mountains. In fact, they're about 20 percent smaller, making them approximately the same size as a husky. Coastal wolves come in all colors, from black to white, but most have reddish-colored fur that's coarser and less dense than the fur on wolves in colder climates. Besides being smaller and redder, sea wolves swim more than any other kind of wolf—a lot more. They're completely content to swim from one island to another in the Great Bear Rainforest as they search for food. Some wolves have been known to swim as far as eight miles (thirteen kilometers) in a day!

CREW QUIP:

When I got out there, I was just so happy with how quiet it was. It's not so much quiet-you-hear-nothing, but quiet-you-hear-nothing-manmade. The other thing was the proximity to wildlife. Because there's not many people around, the wildlife seemed to be closer. So the Steller's jays are closer, the squirrels are closer, the ravens are closer and, of course, the bears are closer. You can be on one side of the river and there's a bear walking on the other side of the river.

—Tim Archer, sound designer

A MEMORABLE FIRST ENCOUNTER

On her first trip to assist with the filming of *Great Bear Rainforest*, Deirdre Leowinata recalls that one day Ian took her to look for wolves on a nearby island. When they arrived, Ian suggested they walk across the island toward a small lagoon. All of a sudden, an alpha wolf walked right up to them! It surprised Deirdre, who had never seen a wolf that close. Ian, however, wasn't fazed: he's been observing and photographing this particular pack of sea wolves for more than twenty years.

"She was six feet [two meters] away from us at one point," Deirdre recalls. "I had never experienced anything like it before. I studied wolves for a summer, but I only saw one from a helicopter."

The wolf circled the pair a couple of times, checking them out, and then it disappeared back into the forest. Deirdre was left feeling completely awestruck for the remainder of their walk, the image of the wolf's beautiful white-grey face etched in her mind. "I didn't realize until months later that Ian was actually just testing me to see if I could handle being in the field," Deirdre laughs. "We weren't walking for any particular reason. He just wanted to see whether I could keep up with him!"

Coastal wolves are genetically, morphologically and behaviorally distinct from mainland wolves.

Like black bears and grizzly bears, wolves are an umbrella species in the Great Bear Rainforest. Umbrella species tend to be large animals with wide ranges. They share the same sorts of requirements as other species in their territories, so protecting an umbrella species also protects other species.

Highly social and intelligent, coastal wolves have been isolated by the vast Coast Mountain range that separates the Great Bear Rainforest from the rest of North America. Unfortunately, wolves on the eastern side of these mountains have suffered centuries of trapping, poisoning and government-sponsored killing, resulting in much of their historic genetic diversity being lost.

In the Great Bear Rainforest, coastal wolves have not been persecuted to the same extent. Because of their relative isolation, they have also kept most of their historic genetic diversity. The combination of genetics, morphology (shape, size) and behavior (living off the ocean) makes coastal wolves unique in the world.

DID YOU KNOW?

In 2016 a tugboat towing a fuel barge ran aground near Bella Bella, a community of about 1,500 in the Great Bear Rainforest. Thankfully the barge was empty at the time of the crash—but more than 26,000 gallons (100,000 liters) of diesel fuel leaked out of the tugboat. That's about as much liquid as a train tanker car can hold, and it spread across nine salmon rivers, eighteen cockle beds, fifty-six clam beds and an endangered abalone bed. Those rivers and shores are also home to halibut, crabs, prawns, shrimp, oysters, sea cucumbers, herring and seaweed—all of which are food sources for the Heiltsuk people.

Years later, the Heiltsuk people still cannot harvest from their traditional shellfish beds in the area.

The coastal wolves have lived side by side with humans throughout history in the Great Bear Rainforest. They are not feared, nor are they hunted by the forest's First Nations people (although non-Indigenous people still hunt them, which threatens their populations). In fact, the sea wolves have long been admired by their human neighbors: First Nations understand that the wolves have every right to share the rainforest with them, and they reflect this belief in their art and stories.

Because they rely on the ocean for food, sea wolves are threatened by anything that threatens the ocean's health. Oil spills, declining salmon stocks and a warming ocean all represent challenges to their existence.

Sound designer Tim Archer smiles during an interview with Kitasoo/Xai'Xais Chief Councillor Douglas Neasloss.

Sibling bears huddle together while their mother fishes nearby.

ANOTHER CREATURE OF THE FOREST that has lived side by side with humans for thousands of years is the bear. Grizzly, black and the rare spirit bears all call this place home—it is, after all, the Great Bear Rainforest, so named because of its largest denizens.

The Great Bear is one of the last places on Earth where bears can live relatively freely, away from human development and exploitation. During the spring and summer, the rainforest bears feast on berries and sedges. In the fall, the salmon return to the rivers and the bears gorge on them, gaining winter stores for the long hibernation ahead. And when winter comes, they bed down in cozy dens, typically in a hollow underneath a giant old-growth tree.

Director Ian McAllister searches for spirit bears.

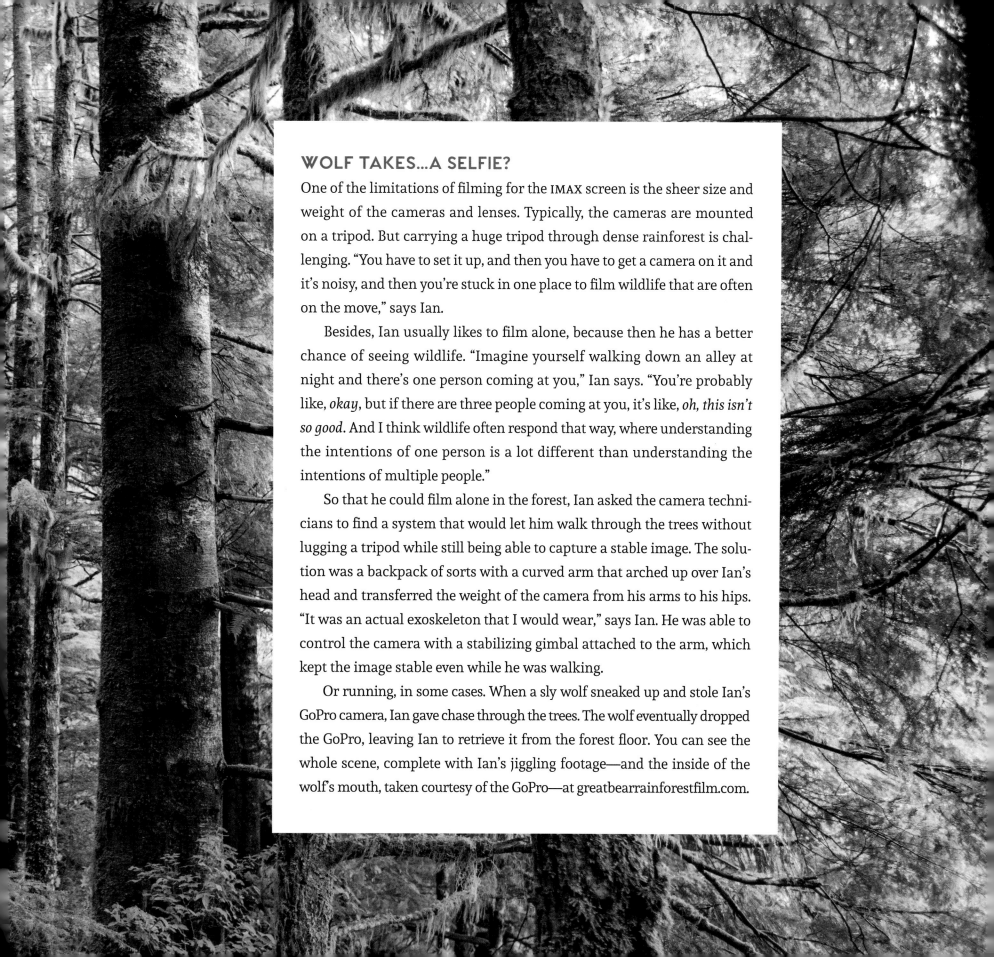

WOLF TAKES...A SELFIE?

One of the limitations of filming for the IMAX screen is the sheer size and weight of the cameras and lenses. Typically, the cameras are mounted on a tripod. But carrying a huge tripod through dense rainforest is challenging. "You have to set it up, and then you have to get a camera on it and it's noisy, and then you're stuck in one place to film wildlife that are often on the move," says Ian.

Besides, Ian usually likes to film alone, because then he has a better chance of seeing wildlife. "Imagine yourself walking down an alley at night and there's one person coming at you," Ian says. "You're probably like, *okay*, but if there are three people coming at you, it's like, *oh, this isn't so good*. And I think wildlife often respond that way, where understanding the intentions of one person is a lot different than understanding the intentions of multiple people."

So that he could film alone in the forest, Ian asked the camera technicians to find a system that would let him walk through the trees without lugging a tripod while still being able to capture a stable image. The solution was a backpack of sorts with a curved arm that arched up over Ian's head and transferred the weight of the camera from his arms to his hips. "It was an actual exoskeleton that I would wear," says Ian. He was able to control the camera with a stabilizing gimbal attached to the arm, which kept the image stable even while he was walking.

Or running, in some cases. When a sly wolf sneaked up and stole Ian's GoPro camera, Ian gave chase through the trees. The wolf eventually dropped the GoPro, leaving Ian to retrieve it from the forest floor. You can see the whole scene, complete with Ian's jiggling footage—and the inside of the wolf's mouth, taken courtesy of the GoPro—at greatbearrainforestfilm.com.

The bears rely on the rainforest for everything in their world. If the old-growth forests on British Columbia's central coast aren't protected, then the bears aren't either—and the whole web of life is forever altered.

Although grizzly bears typically live on the mainland, these forest giants are going hungry as fewer and fewer salmon return to their waterways. In the last few years, grizzlies have begun swimming out to the islands off the central coast in search of food. This is not good news for the black bears (including the spirit bear) that have lived on these islands for thousands of years. Now they are being displaced as the larger, fiercer grizzlies take over their salmon streams.

IN *GREAT BEAR RAINFOREST*, we meet Mercedes Robinson-Neasloss: bear hair researcher, student learner, youth steward of the territory. She received one of her traditional names, Habuk-clamalayu, from her great-grandfather at a Potlatch, where names are traditionally passed on. It means "mother that keeps the family together," and it belonged to

Ian McAllister interviews Kitasoo/Xai'Xais student grizzly-bear technician Mercedes Robinson-Neasloss.

Sedges, grasslike plants found in estuaries, are a critical food for coastal grizzly bears.

her great-grandmother before her. "My grandfather saw in Mercedes the leadership and loving, caring qualities that the name has had," says Mercedes's mother, Roxanne.

The Potlatch tradition—indeed, all the traditions of the Kitasoo/Xai'Xais people, to which Mercedes belongs—is important to Roxanne. She's a teacher of language and culture at the Kitasoo Community School. Haisla and Kitasoo by lineage, Roxanne works with the ten remaining Xai'Xais speakers to keep the language alive.

There are no more native speakers of Sgüüx̱s, the other language once commonly spoken among the Kitasoo peoples, but there are numerous recordings from Roxanne's great-grandmother, who spoke it. A language researcher is working to revitalize that language, so it too can be taught to the children of the Kitasoo Community School.

Mercedes Robinson-Neasloss collects grizzly hairs from a rub tree for DNA analysis.

The passing down of knowledge from one generation to the next—like Roxanne passing the language on to the kids at school—is a cornerstone of First Nations culture. Similarly, Mercedes and other youth in the rainforest are learning from older people about the land and the traditional ways to care for it.

While Mercedes may travel away from the reserve to attend university, Roxanne hopes she will return to share her learning with the community. "I always tell my children you should travel the world and do great things, but that they will always know and have their connection to home," says Roxanne. "And that they go out and aspire to be what they want to be, and come back and offer that to our community so they can inspire others through the work that they're doing, and give back to our people."

WHEN A BEAR WALKS THROUGH YOUR SHOOT

One memorable moment for the film crew was when a grizzly bear walked right through a shoot they'd set up! Douglas, Mercedes and a couple of other researchers were going to be filmed walking along a bear "stomp" trail (that's a very special kind of path where grizzly bears twist their paws as they walk, leaving their scent behind). But one particular grizzly bear had a different idea.

The crew had spent two days setting up the shoot, with an overhead cable-dolly system for one camera, and another camera on a tripod at the end of the trail. Just when Ian called *Action!*, a grizzly bear sauntered right down the trail! Because Douglas, Mercedes and the others were trapped between the bear and the camera crew, they stayed put—and stayed calm. "He wanted his trail," Douglas recalls, "so he starts twisting his paws, doing his territorial marking and moving his head."

The bear skirted the waiting group and proceeded down the trail under the cable cam, straight to the rub tree where the group had been planning to collect bear hairs. Then he began scratching his back on the tree. It was perfect! Both camera crews started rolling, capturing extremely rare footage of a grizzly bear rubbing from above.

The film crew had a once-in-a-lifetime opportunity to film a grizzly bear up close and personal at one of his territorial rub trees.

Researchers can determine sex, diet, stress level and and other information from a single strand of grizzly-bear hair.

Kitasoo/Xai'Xais grizzly-bear researchers travel across the estuary between research sites.

SCIENCE BYTE:
White Wonders of the Forest

The spirit bear is one of the rarest bears in the world and is only found on remote islands in the Great Bear Rainforest. They're not polar bears, nor do they have albinism (a rare condition where an individual lacks pigment). Instead, the spirit bear is the expression of a rare recessive gene among black bears. Black-colored parents can carry the gene, and if they mate with another black-colored bear carrying the recessive gene—or they mate with a spirit bear—there's a chance the resulting offspring will be white. It's similar to how two brown-eyed people can sometimes have a blue-eyed child.

Some scientists think the spirit bear's white color is an advantage when fishing. Imagine you are a salmon looking out for predators. Which will you see more clearly against a white sky: a black bear or a white bear that blends in? An interesting part of this theory is the suggestion of the ocean's importance in this ecosystem being so great that, over hundreds of generations, the bears' color has been changing.

CREW QUIP:

A big part of why I do this type of film work is to help inspire people to care about places and creatures, and as a result be inspired to help protect these places and these creatures. Because you're not inspired to protect something unless you care about it.

—Andy Maser, cinematographer and camera technician

IAN'S WORK WITH PACIFIC WILD, as well as the tireless efforts of Klemtu elected Chief Councillor Douglas Neasloss, helped lead to the eventual end of the grizzly bear trophy hunt in British Columbia in 2017. It took many years of letter writing, petition passing, awareness raising and government lobbying by countless like-minded people until the senseless trophy hunt was banned. After more than a century in the crosshairs, the great bears are no longer being hunted for a rug on someone's wall.

On behalf of coastal First Nations, Douglas was a vocal opponent of the trophy hunt, meeting with leaders in both the provincial and federal governments to discuss the harmful and culturally insensitive practice. "He's got to deal with housing and rights and title court cases and fisheries management, to name just a few of his responsibilities for his community, but he always made sure there was time for the grizzly bear hunt issue," says Ian. "There are so many issues to deal with, with a minister or prime minister. But he would bring up the grizzly hunt time and time again until they were just exhausted. We can be thankful to First Nation leaders like Doug for stopping the hunt."

Now, nobody can shoot a grizzly bear to show off to their friends. The next challenge? Ending the trophy hunt of other large carnivores like black bears and wolves. While there are plenty of black bears in the Great Bear Rainforest, it's impossible to tell which of them carry the rare recessive gene that, when combined with a recessive gene from another black bear, makes a spirit bear.

THE RAINFOREST IS HIGHLY SENSITIVE, and access is carefully managed. To film *Great Bear Rainforest,* the crew needed to develop agreements with local First Nations to ensure that the filming would be done in a sensitive manner while also respecting First Nations culture and interests. A film on the scale of *Great Bear Rainforest* could never have been accomplished without the support of local communities.

Douglas Neasloss was one of the key people in helping create these protocols for filming. Working with bears is something Douglas has been

SNAPSHOT: JEFF TURNER

Home base: Southern interior of British Columbia

Professional handle: Producer, director, writer

Previous jobs: Worked for the CBC on *The Nature of Things* and for the BBC on *Planet Earth*

Role in making the film: Producer, second unit director of photography, aerial photographer

When the bug bit: At age 12 when he began filmmaking with a Super 8 camera his parents bought him

Showed promise: In high school, when he landed film awards in BC and Los Angeles

When the love intensified: During his fish and wildlife technician degree at the BC Institute of Technology, when one of his instructors showed nature documentaries to the class

Claim to fame: In the industry, Jeff is most known for filming bears and wolves, having filmed them all over the world, including in Russia and Alaska and across North America. He's pretty sure he's filmed the spirit bear more than any other person on the planet!

doing for a long time: he helped to start Klemtu's bear tourism in 1999, when he was just seventeen. Tourism is sustainable and non-invasive, unlike many other resource extraction activities such as mining and logging. In the early 1990s, Klemtu faced unemployment rates of over 80 percent, and logging looked like the only way to make a living. In fact, what we now call the Great Bear Rainforest was actually referred to by the provincial government as the North and Mid-Coast Timber Supply Areas.

"Twenty years ago, the main industries for these small remote communities were forestry and fishing," Douglas says. "A lot of companies would come in here and extract everything and then leave. Trying to look at sustainable ways of doing business was extremely important to the community."

Since starting with only two people in 1999, bear tourism in Klemtu now employs about fifty people. Men, women and children all play a role in interpreting their territory for visitors. "We have a lot of respect for bears and we try and give them their space," says Douglas. "We've always shared the estuaries with them—the salmon, the berries and everything in the estuary. They're very important to us, not just for our economy today, but culturally they are very significant, and we're taught to respect them."

LEGENDS OF THE GITGA'AT AND KITASOO First Nations tell how the spirit bear came to be. When Raven created the rainforest after the glaciers receded, he made one of every ten black bears white, as a reminder of a time when snow and ice covered all the land. Equally important in the legend is that Raven created a special, wild place in the world for the spirit bears to live peacefully forever.

Great Bear Rainforest film producer Jeff Turner knows the spirit bears well. He's been filming them and making nature documentaries about them for the CBC and the BBC for decades. In the early 1990s, Jeff, his filmmaker wife, Sue, and their young daughter lived for two years on an island in the Great Bear Rainforest so they could study and film the majestic animals. "In those days only a few even knew the spirit bear existed," says Jeff. "There was no eco-tourism; there was no photography; people had never seen it. There was very little interest or focus on it."

Kitasoo/Xai'Xais Chief Councillor Douglas Neasloss and Mercedes Robinson-Neasloss go through remote camera footage.

That's all changed now. Through his work on films like *Great Bear Rainforest* all the way back to his first documentary, *Island of the Ghost Bear*, Jeff's work has educated and delighted audiences around the world. Many people want to come to the Great Bear Rainforest to see the bears for themselves. And whereas it used to take weeks of waiting to spot a single bear, now more First Nations are running bear-viewing businesses and keeping a closer watch out for the spirit of the forest.

The benefit of community-based wildlife tourism like this is that the revenue goes directly to First Nations communities while providing an incentive to protect the bears' habitat and food supply. It's a win-win for bears and people alike.

New wireless camera technology allowed the crew to film wildlife in a noninvasive way.

FILMING OVER A RIVER

One of the reasons Ian and Jeff were so excited with recent advances in camera technology for IMAX screens was that it allowed them to film animal behavior in a wide variety of hard-to-reach places.

Take bears fishing in a salmon stream, which they were able to capture using a cable and motorized dolly system. "Traditionally, you would have a crew of at least three or four people, not including the people that had to lift the camera and get it into place," says Ian. "You'd have to have a generator. And the sound of the film going through the camera has often been described as being as loud as a Volkswagen Beetle engine."

Loud, cumbersome, heavy—all things that don't lend themselves to experiencing intimate moments with wildlife in a rainforest river valley.

But the new and improved camera gear allowed the *Great Bear Rainforest* crew to set up a long cable along the river and send a camera up by remote control. "Then we could all be downstream," says Ian, "and we had full control over this completely silent camera."

CREW QUIP:

There's lots of waiting in these films. Sometimes if the berries are really good the bears could be off eating berries in the forest and not interested in salmon. You don't always get to see what you've come to see right away. It's a sort of industry where you can spend a week waiting for an amazing ten-minute thing to happen. But that ten-minute thing is so incredible. You know it's going to be in your film. So that makes it all worthwhile at the end.

—Jeff Turner , producer

HE HOLDS THE RESPONSIBILITY OF LOOKING AFTER THE ISLAND WHERE MANY OF THE SPIRIT BEARS LIVE.

Marven Robinson and his son Nelson of the Gitga'at Nation watch a spirit bear fishing for salmon.

Nelson Robinson is learning to be a spirit-bear guide from his father, Marven.

ALL THE SEGMENTS WITH THE SPIRIT BEARS in *Great Bear Rainforest* were filmed with the assistance of Marven Robinson and his son Nelson, who you meet in the film. Marven's family belongs to the Gitga'at First Nation and is part of the Raven Clan. They live in Hartley Bay, a small town in the Great Bear Rainforest with a population of about 160.

Marven has been working with the spirit bears for over twenty years. He now is responsible for managing tourists' access to the bears, and he oversees bear tourism operations in the Gitga'at territories. But how he ended up in that job was a bit of an accident.

After quitting his job as a commercial fisherman in the mid-1990s, Marven returned to Hartley Bay, worried about how he would support his partner and their new baby. In the early morning hours the day after he had returned home, Marven went down to the fueling dock to hang out with his brother. A boat pulled in, and Marven put down his coffee and went to help the driver with the fuel. "You're going to be doing this all day," he said to his brother. "I'll do this first one."

Little did Marven know that the boat's driver was esteemed bear biologist Wayne McCrory. McCrory asked whether Marven knew the chief. It just so happened that Marven did: his girlfriend was the chief's

CREW QUIP:

The theater experience of IMAX is what I think is so wonderful about this, because it's meant to be an immersive experience. It's meant to transport the audience to a world and an experience that they haven't had before. To be in the theater where it will feel like the trees are towering above you, or the mountains are rising and you're flying down this deep, dark valley. It's what it's like to be there. It will really give people a much deeper understanding of the place—of its importance, its beauty, its intactness, why it is so special in the world. And I think it will inspire people to be more concerned about making sure it stays that way.
—Jeff Turner

granddaughter. "He introduced himself and said that he really needed to meet the chief, and he had some things to talk about," says Marven. "It was about the bear. At the time, they called it a ghost bear or a white bear."

After McCrory and Chief Johnny Clifton had their conversation, the chief sent Marven along with McCrory and his team as they went into the forest in search of the elusive "ghost bear."

The small group followed McCrory's dog up a river, until she lay down. "I looked around and I said, *What are we doing listening to a dog?*" Marven recalls. But the group sat patiently in the spot the dog had indicated. "It took about fifteen minutes of us just sitting there," says Marven. "And then out of this little side creek comes this big, beautiful spirit bear. And I've been going ever since."

More than two decades later, Marven is teaching Nelson all he knows about bears. He holds the responsibility of looking after the island where many of the spirit bears live. It was a responsibility given to him by his father-in-law, Chief Johnny Clifton, in the years before the older man died. Now Marven carefully manages all the tours and operators that come to the territory to see the spirit bears. He knows that one day he will pass this responsibility on to Nelson.

For the Gitga'at people, ensuring the protection of the spirit bear is key to ensuring the protection of their territory.

The Coast Mountains form a barrier that isolates the Great Bear Rainforest from the rest of North America.

GETTING A BIRD'S-EYE VIEW

Did you see those soaring panoramic scenes where you're flying along above the mountain peaks, or chasing the water as it sluices down a waterfall? That's aerial filming—and it's one of the things IMAX does best.

In filming *Great Bear Rainforest*'s aerials, the camera was mounted in a Shotover—a large electronic, motorized stabilizer that ensured a smooth picture, even in high-speed situations like helicopter flights. "It's sophisticated in the sense that it's flying along at a hundred miles an hour, sometimes in very rough weather," says Jeff, "and yet the equipment maintains absolute perfect stability."

The Shotover was mounted below the helicopter itself. Jeff sat inside the chopper, in front of a monitor and a control panel so he could control the camera's movements—panning, tilting, zooming, looking to the left or the right, ahead or behind.

Sounds straightforward enough: strap camera on, point, shoot. Right?

Except it isn't. Each time the camera went up in the air, the helicopter pilot, Jeff and Doug Lavender (the camera assistant and IMAX camera technician) had to develop a detailed flight plan ahead of time. They would spend hours figuring out the scene and deciding how the helicopter should move through the scene to best reveal it. Then Jeff and Doug would decide how to move the camera itself within that scene. It's stuff that the filmmakers have been doing for a long time, but it still takes lots of practice and communication with the pilot.

SNAPSHOT: DOUG LAVENDER

How he got his start: Working on *Alive* (1993), a true story about survivors of a plane crash in the Andes. *Alive* was filmed in British Columbia's Purcell Mountains.

Role in making the film: Helping the cinematographers use the large-format ARRI Alexa 65 digital camera, keeping the camera gear organized, assisting with aerial filming

Split personality: Camera assisting on outdoor adventure IMAX films as well as on Hollywood feature films. The best of both worlds!

How he approaches his work: Like a sport. Doug keeps his body strong and flexible so he can cope with the challenging conditions he finds himself in when filming.

Current project: Filming a feature movie called *Scary Stories They Tell in the Dark*

Career advice: Pick role models in your field—people you look up to—and emulate their behavior. Also, lead by example. "You have to do more than what you think is your station in life or your station in your job to inspire others to follow along. You have to be the first one into the river or into the rainstorm to have others follow you."

Producer and cinematographer Jeff Turner takes to the air to capture dramatic landscapes with the IMAX film camera.

FLIPPING FILM ON THE FLY

Because of its size, a 1,000-foot (300-meter) roll will capture only 180 seconds of footage, so Jeff and Doug got only three minutes of shooting each time they went up in the helicopter. (Compare that with a digital camera, where you can pop in a 1-terabyte chip and get an hour of filming.)

When the aerial team had captured their three precious minutes, the helicopter would have to land so they could change the film. They'd rush out and set up a special darkroom tent called a "cat tent," take out the used film, reload the camera with new film, fuel the chopper back up and then take to the skies again.

All told, it was an hour of fussing...for three minutes of filming. "You pick your shots very carefully!" says Jeff.

Large 70 mm film stock—used for shooting aerials—fills this Shotover canister on the front of the helicopter.

Cameraman Andy Maser searches for grizzly bears during a spring shoot.

Filming in the Farthest Corner of the Planet

Camera technician Deirdre Leowinata makes final adjustments
on a jib camera rig while filming humpback whales.

Almost all of the filming for *Great Bear Rainforest* was boat-based.

ECAUSE THE GREAT BEAR RAINFOREST is so remote, most of it is accessible only by water. While filming took place in a variety of locations—on the water, in the air, on the land and under the sea—the one place where everyone regrouped was on the boats. Whether it was dispatching a small Zodiac from one of the larger "mother ships" to take Tim Archer to a quiet island to capture audio or flying a drone from the deck of *Habitat*, almost everything happened from the surface of the water.

"That's a challenge," says Jeff. "When you're dealing with moisture issues in the equipment, lots of rain, getting in and out of places, dealing with high water and tides and all those sorts of things...it brings a level of complexity to filming in this environment."

DID YOU KNOW?

Although most of the film crew had their own cabins aboard *Habitat* and *Canadian Shore*, sometimes deckhands and technicians shared a cabin. This could be tricky: the technicians often came to bed late at night, while the deckhands had to be up before the birds.

CREW QUIP:

On a typical day there are so many things that can go wrong. And if something does, you're often a day or more away from the nearest town. In the wintertime, when we are on dive trips, it's typical not to see another boat or person for a month or even longer. Add in all the hurricane-force storm events, strong currents and snow blizzards, and it makes for some pretty interesting adventures. Being able to fix gear as it breaks and keep all the systems running is a key part of successfully operating on this coast.

—Ian McAllister

DID YOU KNOW?

A herring school will spawn in just a few hours, with females laying up to 6 million eggs per square meter—half a million eggs per square foot. That's a lot of eggs! The eggs incubate for about ten days before they hatch. The best water temperature for them is 50 degrees Fahrenheit (10 degrees Celsius).

TWO BOATS ARE BETTER THAN ONE

Through the critical seasons, when there was a lot of activity in the forest—like in the springtime—both Jeff and Ian would have their own mother ship with crew so they could divide their energies and capture different footage. Ian might be focused on filming the coastal wolves while Jeff captured the spirit bears and their Gitga'at guardians. Then Jeff would head off to film grizzly bears while Ian shifted to focus on the humpback whales. "There's often so much to do at these critical times that we just needed to both be out there," says Jeff.

The Great Bear is also a big place. This meant the crew had to be mobile, able to move around quickly. "You can show up at a place and somebody will say, *Oh, you should have been here yesterday! It was all happening!*" says Jeff. "You're not always in the right spot at the right time, because sometimes it takes a few days to get there."

The herring spawn is a perfect example of the importance of being in the right place at the right time. It took the team three seasons to capture what you see in the film, because the spawn lasts only a few days in many locations. If you miss it, you have to wait twelve months to try again.

Tim Archer patiently records the sounds of sea otters in kelp forests.

The herring spawn in early spring is so important to the Heiltsuk First Nation that it marks the beginning of their new year.

SCIENCE BYTE:
Tiny Giants Supporting the Forest Ecosystem

Except during the great spawning event in the spring, herring are rarely seen. As that special early spring day creeps closer—governed by temperature, lunar cycles and tides—the herring begin roiling up from the deep in gigantic rotating balls.

Many animals, as well as First Nations fishers, take care not to make any sudden noise or movements once the spawn is underway. Herring spook easily, and a gigantic school of them can vanish in the blink of an eye if they take fright.

Where salmon lay their eggs in gravel and then carefully cover their nests, herring take the sea by storm, depositing millions of eggs on seaweed in the near-shore environment. It's a numbers game for the herring: only one in 10,000 will survive to adulthood, so it makes sense to lay gazillions of eggs.

Fatty and rich in nutrients, herring eggs are the caviar of the North Pacific. This little fish has been a critical food source for the people of the Great Bear for millennia. Recent archaeological digs have revealed 6,000-year-old herring bones at some settlement sites! Herring have most likely been more consistently abundant than even salmon for Pacific Northwest cultures.

Being primarily boat-based meant a lot of days spent together in tight quarters. This filming environment, in particular, offered up an extreme version of the challenge of cooperating as a team. They were working in high-pressure situations with wildlife, maintaining a ton of camera gear and packing it in and out of remote places, and sleeping and eating together on a single, small boat on a big ocean. "The most important thing is that you have to be able to get along," says Deirdre, "and if there are differences, you have to be able to work out those differences. Otherwise nothing's going to work well."

Camera technician Deirdre Leowinata configures the wireless system of a cable rig during the spring grizzly shoot.

SNAPSHOT: DEIRDRE LEOWINATA

Professional handle: Camera and digital imaging technician

Role in making the film: Everything logistical, from prepping camera rigs to troubleshooting tech issues to training deckhands to managing chaos

Previous jobs: Production coordination and management, data management, camera assistant

Childhood dream: To save the world

Formal schooling: Biology degree with a focus on conservation and climate change

Owes her inspiration to: Dr. Jeremy Kerr, an ecology professor who studies climate change through butterflies

Bragging rights: Being able to quickly prep multiple rigs including the drone, cable dolly, underwater and topside cameras. "I was comfortable switching those rigs really fast, and troubleshooting. That became kind of my specialty."

Near-death experience (the camera's, not hers): When the crew had set up a cable dolly over a creek bed and the carabiner snapped. Thankfully the creek was at low tide, so the camera avoided water damage!

SALT WATER WOES

Filming in a coastal rainforest meant the crew was dealing with salt water at every turn. That's a drag, because salt water can destroy camera equipment, fast. Salt locks up gears and joints, rendering equipment useless. Even salt air can create problems. "Salt water is the bane of my existence," moans Deirdre, who was largely responsible for taking care of the equipment. "I'd rather climb a mountain in a desert."

The crew had to make sure they always kept the cameras and other equipment spanking clean and locked away in cases when it wasn't in use. At the end of every season, the crew would carefully apply corrosion-blocking solutions to all the teeny-tiny metal parts, especially on the drone. This helped to ensure that everything was in good working order at the start of the next season.

For the most part, the crews aboard *Habitat* and *Canadian Shore* got along well. Naturally there were times when people grew a little stressed if the technology wasn't working properly, but in general the work environment was harmonious—especially once a crew had worked together for several weeks and had developed trusted habits.

The boats would head out for at least two months at a time, usually with four to five crew members. This meant stocking up and planning ahead.

The crew operates a heavy lift drone from the deck of *Habitat*. From left to right: director Ian McAllister, cinematographer Andy Maser, drone pilot Brian Dalrymple and camera technician Deirdre Leowinata.

CREW QUIP:

With microphones, you've got to be very careful. I try and keep them in foam packaging and out of the elements. With digital recorders, I don't. I'll leave these in the pouring rain and I'll come back and I'll just shake them and make them work. What I do is I strap [a digital recorder] to a tree and then I cover the battery and most of it in a rain poncho. I'll wrap that around a tree and then I'll put a hood on it, of sorts. But if it gets wet, the card's great. The card's not going to fail, so I'll get my recording. My gear gets pretty beat up and it keeps on ticking.

—Tim Archer

Sound designer Tim Archer adjusts the audio while recording the Kitasoo/Xai'Xais grizzly-bear researchers.

STORM SURGE

You know you're in brutal conditions when you've got both engines pinned dead ahead, wild winds whipping all around you and 350 feet (100 meters) of anchor chain out—and you're still being pushed backwards. That's what the crew of *Habitat* weathered one day during herring season, right after Ian returned from a dive. "I was just scuba diving one minute, and then I pop my head up and there's all these whitecaps," he recounts in the behind-the-scenes trailer. "We just barely managed to get to the boat before the storm hit."

Good thing it was daytime: if that storm had hit at night, Ian figures that things would not have turned out so well. "Every time one of the major gusts came, I was able to see when the water picked up," he says. "And then I'd kind of point the boat into it. But if it had been at night, I would not have been able to see where the weather was coming from. A few broadsides of those 80-plus-knot gusts and I think we would have been on the rocks."

The crew had known ahead of time that the forecast was for a short, intense system. But they didn't expect it to be quite so ferocious. "In Bella Bella, docks fell over," Ian recalls. "Boats sank and telephone poles fell on houses. All kinds of damage."

WHILE THERE WAS NO "TYPICAL DAY" during the shooting, the crew established a pattern for how the time unfolded. In the summertime, long daylight hours made it possible to film between 4:00 AM and 10:00 PM, so the team had to be careful not to work too much and burn themselves out. During those long days, the deckhand (who was quite often the cook as well) would be the first person awake—usually by about 3:45 in the morning. The coffee was hot by the time the crew rolled out of bed, and breakfast had to be ready so that everyone could pile into the Zodiacs by 5:00 and head for the day's shoot. If there wasn't time to eat, the cook/deckhand would try to pack a thermos of coffee and something yummy for the trip. And every now and again, a superstar deckhand would drop by a day-long shoot with a bag full of snacks.

CREW QUIP:

Jeff Turner had told me early on that the best thing to wear is chest-waders. So whether it's rain or shine, you get into your chest-waders first thing in the morning. And you wear them all day, because in the rainforest, sometimes the best path is up the streambed. Because everywhere else, there's huge logs the size of cars and all these slippery rocks and huge gnarled branches in front of you. So sometimes the best way to walk is straight up the river or stream you're trying to explore.
—Doug Lavender

Camera operator Jeff Turner and film assistant Doug Lavender wait for a spirit bear to appear.

Being boat-based meant crew members had to have multiple skill sets. Deckhand Haley Crozier holds a monitor for drone pilot Brian Dalrymple while Andy Maser operates the camera for a drone aerial.

NOT ANOTHER GRANOLA BAR!

While you might be thinking the crew was stuck eating moldy rice by the end of every journey into the field, they actually ate rather well. "Sometimes you're bringing food back from the ocean on a dive," says Ian. "We ate a lot of seafood. Salmon, cod, prawns, sea cucumbers, geoducks and crabs."

But some of the food grew tiresome. "Man, we lived off granola bars and I don't know what else," says Deirdre. "Nuts. I got so sick of those little chocolate-covered fruits. You just get to that point where you can't eat another chocolate-covered blueberry."

One important bit of work was to prep all the gear the night before so there were no surprises in the morning. It was not uncommon for some of the crew to work late into the night, trying to troubleshoot a piece of gear. And there were a lot of systems: the topside rig (a camera on a tripod with a long lens on it), one or two drones and their rigs, the underwater camera kit and strobe lights, the gimbals, the behind-the-scenes kit, the cable-dolly kit, the time-lapse kit. And batteries, batteries, batteries: for camera lights, camera strobes, scooters, dive alarms and more.

Cameras, lenses, filters, tripods...for every shoot there was a heap of gear to load into a Zodiac—sometimes even two. On top of that, if rain was in the forecast, the crew would pack tarps and umbrellas as well.

CREW QUIP:

With only four of us going into the forest every day, one of the challenges was trying to figure out how to get all the equipment we needed into four backpacks. On the way [to the Great Bear] I was organizing backpacks and trying to strategize how to get everything we needed into those four backpacks. Because once you leave the boat in the morning...we wouldn't come back till 6:00. I had everything all figured out and I'm like, *Okay, perfect! We've got four backpacks, four people, we're good!* And then we're like, *Wait a minute, what are we going to eat and drink all day?* So we had to put everything into three backpacks. Because we needed one backpack just for food and for water and toilet paper and a tarp.

—Doug Lavender

CREW QUIP:
We had a rain cover that went over the camera, but it was super awkward because it wasn't really made for that system. So most of the time you'd just have somebody standing next to you holding an umbrella over you and the camera. Which is also very awkward.
—Andy Maser

Cable dollies were used to mount cameras for intimate moments and tough angles. Brian Dalrymple and Logan Turner get the camera ready to capture bears fishing for salmon at a waterfall.

The deckhand helped load the boat, and then the crew was off, motoring toward the shore. Sometimes the deckhand would drop the crew off and head back to the mother ship for the day, returning at sundown to bring everyone home again. This was a great setup, because the film crew wouldn't have to worry about keeping an eye on their Zodiac as the tides changed.

Once ashore (or underwater), the magic began!

SO YOU THINK YOU WANT TO BE A DECKHAND?

Okay, here's the gig: You're up with the sun, cooking for the crew. (You darn well better make sure there's coffee, too, especially on Ian's boat.) Speaking of boats, you'll be helping out with that—a lot. That means helping with leaving the dock, getting back to the dock, getting fuel, making sure all the jerry cans are full and having the Zodiacs ready to go. *That* means making sure they're emptied of water, the engines are working and there's gas in them. Sounds like a lot? Hold on, there's more. You'll be the one sitting for hours at a time up in the wheelhouse, in the wind or the cold or the scorching sun, watching out for logs and yelling back to the crew if there's wildlife to be filmed. Oh, and you'll get even less sleep than everyone else on the boat. Ready? Okay, go!

Shotover technician Benjamin Goertzen builds and balances the stabilizer rig before mounting it on *Habitat*.

Sound designer Tim Archer waits for the cue to record.

CREW QUIP:

I never make a mistake that anybody will catch. I make a lot of mistakes, yes, but I won't get caught because I am, as my dad calls it, a belt-and-suspenders kind of guy. If I need two batteries, I'll have six. I know that if my main recorder dies, I've got a backup that'll do exactly what [the first one] does. I've got a backup to that that'll do 90 percent of what [the second one] does. So I will always get the recording that I need. Because when I get back to the studio, if I don't have the recording, it's my fault.

—Tim Archer

Great Bear Rainforest took almost three years to film—much longer than your typical Hollywood movie! That's because the wildlife is spread across an enormous, constantly changing landscape. It's different from other movies where the actors live on set in trailers, ready to shoot according to a precise schedule. That's just not the way wildlife rolls.

DANGER IN THE NIGHT

The Great Bear Rainforest is a temperate rainforest, which means it doesn't really get scorching hot (like, say, the Amazon does). Nor does it undergo deep freezes like they have on the prairies. But that's not to say winter doesn't blow its chilly breath into the river valleys from time to time. One night a winter storm blew up, causing Ian's boat, *Habitat*, to drag its anchor. The three crew on board sprang into action—in their pajamas. "We all had to work together because Ian had to run the engines to keep the boat away from shore, which is hard at night, especially in a snowstorm," says Deirdre.

Because radar and chart plotters don't work when it's snowing so hard, the only way Ian could tell which way he had to go was to watch the snow as it fell, point the boat into it, and gun the engines. "The anchor winch, the windlass, wasn't working...it was pretty stressful," recalls Deirdre, who helped deckhand Haley Crozier shovel five inches (about thirteen centimeters) of snow off the deck once morning broke. "He still talks about how touch and go it was that night. I don't know if he's being dramatic or not, but I feel like he's kind of not, because he's been doing this for so long."

Ian McAllister and Andy Maser film a black bear and other wildlife after a massive mudslide engulfed a salmon river during the IMAX shoot.

Deckhand Haley Crozier dresses for the weather during a coastal blizzard.

While the camera crew moved as a unit most of the time, keeping close tabs on one another and working as a coordinated team, there was one crew member who often was found far from the group, wandering solo on the beaches and along the streambeds. That lone ranger was Tim Archer, whose job it was to capture sound for every part of the film.

You see, shooting a movie in a rainforest involves a lot of filming in areas where there's a lot of rushing water. Most of the bear footage was shot along the banks of streams—which makes for a great *picture*, but not much in terms of actually hearing what the bear is doing. The camera lenses can zoom from a far distance, but a mic? Well, nobody has yet invented a "long lens" for a microphone.

CREW QUIP:

The first time you see a spirit bear it's mind-blowing, really. I knew sooner or later I was going to see one. You're waiting and then, you know, finally when you do, you don't even bother recording because it's like, *No, no, this is my moment. I'm going to see them a lot, and this is just for me.* It's awesome.

—Tim Archer

Andy Maser hard at work filming wolves during the salmon-spawn shoot.

So Tim had to figure out ways to capture the sound without getting all that noise from the rivers and streams. When Jeff suggested they visit a fishing hole that one particular bear frequented, Tim jumped at the chance. The hole was at a relatively quiet part of the river, which meant Tim would have a shot at capturing some real-life sounds produced by a black bear while fishing. He positioned himself behind a tree near the bear's fishing hole and prayed that the bear would show up.

It did. After a sidelong glance at Tim and a sniff of his fuzzy microphone, the bear waded into the water, pulled out a salmon, dropped it on a log and, to Tim's astonishment and glee, proceeded to tear into it. "What they normally do is they pull the salmon up," he says. "They'll take the brains or eggs and leave the rest. But he tore the *whole thing* apart! I think he did it for me."

It got even better: the bear actually caught—and ate—three full salmon while Tim goggled from the streambank. "You wouldn't believe the sound," he says. "I mean, the *crack*, the *rip*—all these sounds!" For Tim, it was worth the mosquito bites and cramped arms as he held the mic close.

MAMA BEAR, UP CLOSE AND PERSONAL

Picture this: It was the end of a long day of shooting in the fall, and the crew was tired. Ian and his gang were ready to head back to *Habitat*, so Deirdre headed back to the area where the crew had been filming to gather up the last few bags. Along the way, she spotted a mother grizzly with a three-year-old cub in tow. Knowing that grizzly bears can sometimes be unpredictable, Deirdre chose to stop walking and wait quietly for the duo to pass.

The mother bear kept walking—straight toward Deirdre. "It was the most awe-inspiring moment," Deirdre recalls. When the grizzly sow was about ten feet (three meters) away—close enough that Deirdre could see the pupils of her eyes—she turned suddenly and headed in a different direction. Her cub followed suit.

Working with wildlife requires patience, trust, understanding and good judgment. Working on *Great Bear Rainforest* has taught the crew about more than just the world of the grizzly. "You definitely learn about yourself," muses Deirdre. "I've learned a lot about myself over the past couple years."

Spirit bears can be born from black or white mothers.

Ravens and wolves have a long-standing symbiotic relationship, both ecologically and in First Nations culture.

WAITING FOR THE WOLVES

It was late days in the wolf shoot, and Tim was beginning to worry. He'd been out for two solid weeks, but he hadn't yet captured any audio of a wolf howling. He was panicking: he only had two days left before he had to leave for his daughter's wedding. What if he didn't get any wolves?

In the pre-dawn hours on the morning before Tim was scheduled to fly out, the radio crackled to life on *Canadian Shore*, informing the crew that a wolf howl had been pinpointed on one of the local islands. Discouraged, Tim went back to sleep: his recorder was strapped to a tree on a different island. No chance of getting that howl.

In the morning, though, he asked a boat driver to take him and his gear to the island where the wolf howl had been reported in hopes of capturing some wolf sound bites. He strapped his recorder to a tree and set off for the beach with additional recording gear and a tripod.

"So I'm walking on the beach by myself," Tim recalls, "and walking right toward me is a big male wolf. And I put the tripod down. And I hit record."

Thirty feet (ten meters) away the wolf stopped and looked at Tim, then looked away, toward a nearby island. "I figured he was going to jump in the water and swim away, or he was going to go back into the forest where he came from," Tim says. "And I'm looking at him and I said to him, *Look, buddy, you've gotta howl for me. I'm leaving tomorrow, literally. This is my last day. You've got to howl.*"

The wolf looked back at Tim, then turned to walk away. "And as he's turning to walk away, he lifts his head and just howls," Tim says. "And I've got a microphone pointing right at him, and the surround mic and the digital recorder off in the distance in the trees, *all* recording. And from everywhere, ravens come in and start circling around him and yelling at him. So if you're in the IMAX theater, they're in the roof. And he's in the middle."

The wolf gave Tim seven howls over the course of eight minutes. When he was finished, he walked straight toward Tim and then past him, watching him the whole time. "Then he gets in the water and swims away. It was just unbelievable," Tim says. "The next thing I hear is Ian on my radio: [*crackle*] *Yeah, are you guys out there?* And I'm like, *Yeah. Ian, I can go home now. I got it.*"

Filming in a remote wilderness setting presented challenges at every turn. But by working together, using common sense, drawing on their combined expertise and taking risks when the right opportunities presented themselves, the *Great Bear Rainforest* crew captured this magical place in a way no humans have ever done before.

"We had three years to shoot," says Ian, reflecting on the experience of bringing the Great Bear's teeming wilderness to a worldwide audience. "Essentially what I wanted in this film was the very best of what I had experienced over my thirty years of working on research and wildlife conservation projects." Now that the film has arrived on the giant screen, it seems that this dream has come true.

Grizzly bear cubs grow up together, only leaving their mothers after three years. These yearling cubs feed on spawned-out salmon.

> "ESSENTIALLY WHAT I WANTED IN THIS FILM WAS THE VERY BEST OF WHAT I HAD EXPERIENCED OVER MY THIRTY YEARS OF WORKING ON RESEARCH AND WILDLIFE CONSERVATION PROJECTS."
> —IAN McALLISTER

The Kitasoo/Xai'Xais grizzly-bear researchers pose for a photo with the crew after a long day of filming. During shoots, crew members spent 24 hours a day together for up to two months at a time.

A Final Word

I T WAS ONLY ABOUT TWENTY-FIVE YEARS AGO
that the Great Bear Rainforest was formally designated a Timber Supply
Area or TSA by the British Columbia government. In their eyes it was a
place so remote and inconsequential that it was only good for one thing:
supplying trees, fish and other raw resources to the outside world. Back
then, few people outside the Great Bear's borders knew it existed, and
even fewer knew of the First Nations people who have occupied its rich,
treed wilderness for over 14,000 years.

But that was then. As more and more people learned about the fabled
rainforest, and the bears and wolves and people who call it home, more
and more voices spoke out for its protection. First Nations communities patiently but forcefully kept reminding the Canadian and British
Columbia governments that their rights and title have never been surren-
dered, and that protecting their traditional territories is vital to their
culture and history.

It has been an extraordinary evolution. Humans rarely, if ever, take
steps to protect a place that's unknown to them. We defend and protect

CREW QUIP:
I wanted the film to be told through the voice
of First Nations people, in particular the new
generation of youth leaders who are responsible
for so many of the positive changes happening
on this coast.
—Ian McAllister

what we know, what we love and what we understand. But that isn't true of the Great Bear Rainforest. Because it's so remote, few people have ever traveled to this magnificent coast—but that hasn't stopped them from caring about it. Just the thought of it in all its natural splendor has been enough to spur people from all over Canada and the world to tell their government representatives that the Great Bear Rainforest matters. That the birds and animals who live in it matter. And that the people who call it home matter too.

Much has been done to protect the Great Bear Rainforest since its designation as a TSA, but there is still much to do to bring back the abundance that once characterized this coast. Wild salmon, whales, herring and many other species all need conservation attention. And we humans need reminding of what we stand to lose if we don't continue to safeguard this wilderness. We hope—the people who worked on this IMAX hope—that the film gives viewers a glimpse of how precious but also how fragile the Great Bear Rainforest is. We hope the film shows the richness, both ecologically and culturally, of the rainforest, and also inspires greater public participation in its protection.

Protecting the environment is not "someone else's job"—it's everyone's duty. Each and every one of us can make a difference when it comes to healing the planet. That's true of the Great Bear Rainforest too. You may not live in it or even near it, but that doesn't mean your voice doesn't count in saving it. If you should be fortunate enough to visit the Great Bear wilderness one day, enjoy it. Be inspired by it. Let it take your breath away. Together, let's ensure it remains one of the most spectacular and awe-inspiring places on Earth.

"IT'S IMPORTANT FOR THE general public to know this is a very special place to a lot of people and that the Heiltsuk are open to inviting people in as long as they're conducting themselves in a good way. And as long as we're ensuring that the future generations of all people and all humanity get to experience the beauty of our territory. It's a special place, not just to us but to a lot of people. So we know that we have guarded it jealously and put measures in effect to ensure that we take care of it, but it's because we care. We love this place. And we literally are the ocean and land that we come from. And I feel that I have a deep spiritual connection to this place. I could talk to you about where my ancestors are buried. I could talk to you about how I go out and hunt seals and take herring and literally eat off the land and have this deep relationship to this place. And we want to keep that, and we think it's in the best interest of everyone if we're the ones who are at the helm and actually managing it and making decisions that affect the people who know it best. And that's us...We know this place best, and if you want to actually make some real conservation efforts, come to talk to the people here since time began."

—Saul Brown

For more information

Have you been inspired by the Great Bear Rainforest? If so, maybe you would like to join the growing effort to protect it. If this Pacific paradise is going to have a safe future, now is the time to add your voice.

Pacific Wild is a nonprofit conservation organization that works to protect wildlife in this important coastal wilderness. Pacific Wild supports innovative research, public education, community development and global awareness to achieve the goal of lasting wildlife protection. A portion of the royalties earned from the sale of this book will support Pacific Wild's work.

For more information on the Great Bear Rainforest or to learn how to support Pacific Wild's conservation work, please contact us at:

Pacific Wild
PO Box 26
Denny Island, BC V0T 1B0
Canada
info@pacificwild.org · pacificwild.org

@pacificwild   facebook.com/PacificWild.org   @pacificwild

INDEX

*Page numbers in **bold** indicate an image caption.*

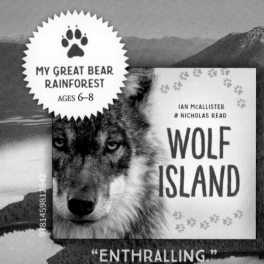

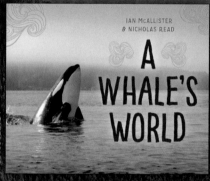
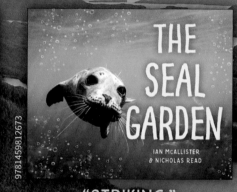
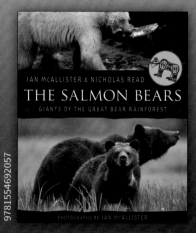
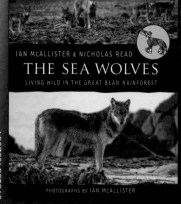

Alaska

Haida
Gwaii

GREAT BEAR
RAINFOREST

Pacific Ocean

Vancouver
Island